The Power of LET-GO

SHARAM

EDITED BY
Shahed & Nafiseh

TALIA

THE POWER OF LET-GO
SHARAM

Edited by: Shahed & Nafiseh
Paperback 1st Edition
Published in 2018 by:

Talia, Friends of Existence, Inc.
Website: www.taliafriends.org
Email: talia@taliafriends.org

Copyright © 2018 by Talia, Friends of Existence, Inc.
ISBN 978-0-9600047-0-6

All rights reserved.
No part of this book may be reproduced, stored in a retrieval system, or transmitted in any form or by any means, electronic, mechanical, photocopying, recording or otherwise, without the prior written permission of the publisher.

Many thanks to Melina H & Stefan Hoelscher for their invaluable help.
Cover Art & Paintings: Sharam

More Books
by Sharam

Order now on:
SharamLove.com

Don't Beat Yourself Up

You Are Your Happiness

The Book of Existence
Part One

Mysticism
The Psychology of Love

Happiness
The Essence of Your Being

Decoding Love
Understanding is Compassion

From Negativity to Joy

THE GLOSSARY

While reading,
if you come across
a mystical concept
you are unfamiliar with,
there is a glossary
at the end of the book
for reference.

INTRODUCTION

Simplicity is the whole message of mysticism. *The Power of Let-Go* is a simple book that really doesn't need an introduction. Read it with the simplicity of your heart, letting the complexity of the mind step aside. If you are wondering how to get in touch with your heart, don't worry, it is very simple. Hopefully, when you read each page, your heart will open automatically.

We are always afraid of our own negativity. We want to hide it. Because of this, these negativities create distance between us and us. If we let our negativities surface with someone who is loving and non-judgmental, we can look at them and come to understand ourselves more. Gradually, these negativities drop and we come closer to ourselves and others.

When you are aware, in that moment the heart opens and you feel one with others. When the heart opens, you accept automatically. So awareness brings acceptance. The reverse is also true. When you accept someone or something, you bring awareness to yourself and your heart opens. When this happens, energy gets stored in the heart and turns into love. Awareness is always attached to acceptance. These two are always together.

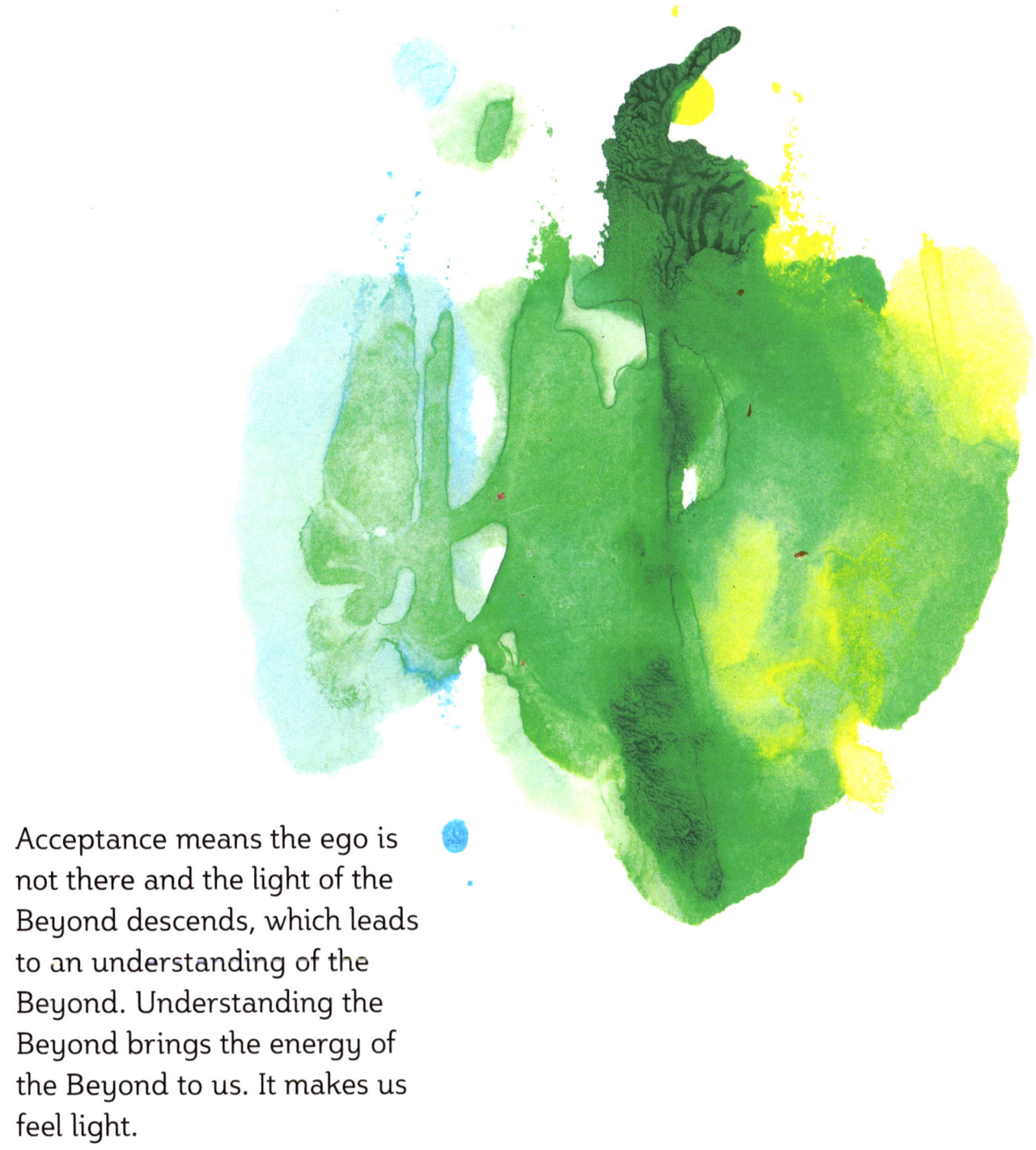

Acceptance means the ego is not there and the light of the Beyond descends, which leads to an understanding of the Beyond. Understanding the Beyond brings the energy of the Beyond to us. It makes us feel light.

Everyone is living in an illusion. Why? We want to believe that we are only good, that we have no bad in us at all. Because of this and according to what we have been taught is good and bad, we only acknowledge certain things about ourselves and try to hide the rest. And because we don't want to see our own negativity, we defend ourselves to the max. The truth is that there is no good and bad. All suffering comes from trying to hide or avoid what we believe is bad. We need to look at our negativity over and over until one day we see it, through and through. When this happens, it will not have a hold on us anymore.

There is no such thing as somebody putting us down in the inner world. We can't go lower than where we are. We create high and mighty images of ourselves, so when someone criticizes us, we feel we have been pulled down from our pedestal and get upset. We just have to let go of our illusions. That is the best thing people on the path of self-discovery can do for themselves.

The ego feeds on negativity. We have been taught that if we think we are good, then we get a big ego. In reality, it is the opposite. If we think we are good, the ego steps aside. It is only when we think we are not good, consciously, unconsciously, or both, that our ego becomes big. It is only when deep inside, you think you are not good enough, that your ego needs to become big to prove how great it is. So the ego feeds on negativity.

If you can accept yourself, you can love yourself and others will love you too. Every time we don't accept, we feel guilty. This guilt is very subtle and very harmful. Every time we don't like something, we also don't accept ourselves, because deep inside we know that we are rejecting Existence. We reject ourselves for rejecting Existence. We are hating and not accepting ourselves, but this is so subtle that we don't know we are doing it. The manifestations of self-hatred are pushing people away, being harsh, being angry and nasty. So not accepting creates guilt and guilt creates judgment and hate. When we don't accept ourselves, we destroy our energy and become harsh and judgmental, all because our energy is eaten up by guilt. It is the same as being in a rush. When you are in a rush, your lose energy. That is why you become easily agitated and angry. All we want is love, but Existence says first you have to accept yourself, love yourself. When you love yourself, you become lovable. Then everybody else loves you too.

Not accepting ourselves is just a habit. A habit is something you do that you are not aware of. If you bring awareness to your habits, they are no longer habits. So one good way to love yourself is to watch your non-acceptance of yourself.

Negativity can be either subtle or not-so-subtle (gross). Some people may seem more negative than others; the slightest thing can set them off, and they express their negativity freely. Their negativity has more energy behind it so it comes out easily or harshly. It is more gross. In others, negativity is there, but it doesn't come out on a regular basis. It only comes out when the person is under a great deal of pressure, or feels a great injustice has been done to them. Their negativity is more subtle. But we need to know that negativity is negativity, and it doesn't matter whether it is gross or subtle; we still need to look at and accept it. When it is gross, it is much easier to look at. If our negativity is subtle: we need to be more subtle and not get fooled into thinking we are not negative, because then we won't see our negativity, and seeing is everything if you want to get rid of negativity.

Thinking consumes a lot of our energy, but if we accept our thinking and are total in it, it won't consume our energy. Whatever we do, if we do it totally, we conserve energy and the sum of all these energies will bring transformation to us. The mind will stop. Also, if we have acceptance we save energy.

Feeling awkward means something has changed and we don't accept it.

Existence knows exactly what we need and whatever is happening in this moment is exactly what we need right now. Everything has its time. Our growth happens exactly when it should, when we are ready, and not one minute before or after. Everything is so exact in Existence, it is absolutely mind-boggling!

The Beyond has a healing effect on both our chakras and the layers of our soul. Karma is made in the etheric body, where the chakras are located. The etheric body sits between the physical body and the emotional body. When karma travels to the emotional body, it blocks the flow of energy to the emotional body, causing weakness there. Then, because of this weakness, you experience a lot of negative emotions. One of the biggest builders of weakness in the emotional body is comparison. With comparison we cannot be happy with what we have and who and where we are. We think others have it better than we do, all because of karma in our emotional bodies. These negative emotions like, "I am not good enough, they are better than me, or they have things that I don't have," bring up desires in us and we want more and more. All of this creates tension in the emotional body. It creates anxiety, worrying, and disharmony in our minds and our lives and takes us to the future.

Acceptance washes away tensions. When you accept something deeply, you open the door to the Beyond and tons of healing energy pours into the chakras and every layer of your soul—the physical, the etheric, the emotional and the mental layers— cleansing them of tension and karma. The only thing that can heal emotional issues and scars, chakra blockages, and other problems is acceptance.

So watch your non-accepting mind. Watch the fact that the mind wants to complain and is not happy with what is. We call this not accepting. Get a pen and paper and write down throughout the day how many times you are rejecting or comparing. Pay attention to when you are not liking something or when your mind is telling you this is not right. Existence is happening in these moments, but we are rejecting it. If you can catch yourself comparing twenty times in a row and instead accept them each time, your comparison will stop forever. Even if you only catch your comparison, but cannot accept it, it will help you a lot. So paying attention also works, it just takes longer.

Acceptance is divine. It is the door to the Beyond. It heals the chakras, and heals each layer of your soul. For acceptance, you have to watch. That means you have to become aware. Awareness and acceptance go together. If you are not aware, how will you know what to accept?

If people are not loving towards us, it is just our reflection coming back to us from Existence. If we can see that we are the one who is not loving, the door to the Beyond opens for us. We just have to look at ourselves without judgment. When we judge, the door to the Beyond closes to us. Judgment, blame, any negativity closes the door to the Beyond or Existence or God.

We can live our lives in one of two ways. One is like a dead person, the other is to live a life that is alive and full of magical experiences. When our energy is low, the Beyond doesn't happen. There are so many things that cause low energy— eating dead food, not chewing our food enough, worrying, blaming, negative emotions, hating ourselves, on and on. When the door to the Beyond closes, there is no magic. And believe me, we need the Beyond for any kind of healing, for experiencing life, and really being alive. We are here on this planet: shouldn't we be really alive?

Love is always young. Why?
Because, every time you feel
love, you visit the Beyond. When
you catch your mind,
you visit the Beyond also.
When we visit the Beyond,
we come to the moment, to the
here and now, and being in the
moment always refreshes us,
makes us alive and really happy.

What is the difference between intensity and passion? Passion is from the second chakra. It is impure; it has emotions involved in it. Intensity is pure; it is from the fifth chakra. There are no emotions involved in it. With anything impure we need not worry. It is a great opportunity to work on ourselves to refine and purify that thing.

Love starts in the fourth chakra, the heart, but it becomes pure in the fifth chakra, the throat. What does it mean to have pure love? When your love is pure, you don't get easily upset over things. You stay centered and accept others completely. The more clean your fifth chakra, the more pure your love will be. So how do we clean our fifth chakra? Singing! Singing clears the throat, allowing our energy to move beyond the fifth chakra to the sixth, and in the sixth, when it is cleansed, we feel unity with everything and everybody. There are many other ways to cleanse our fifth chakra. For example, understanding ourselves cleanses this chakra. Breathing exercises and many movements of yoga are to cleanse this chakra, as well as many other exercises that are made for this or any chakra.

One law of Existence is that if you don't love yourself, others won't love you either, because if they love you, and deep inside you feel unworthy of it, somehow you will punish yourself. Usually, we avoid this by unconsciously creating situations so that they don't love us in the first place.

Guilt creates a dark halo around the heart chakra. This dark halo causes misery, suffering and disease. So many issues come from guilt— disease, discomfort, money issues, friendship issues, greed. Even issues like writer's block and thinking that we are not good enough all come from guilt. When we feel guilty, we feel we are not good enough, and then good things don't happen for us. Even if, by accident, we end up with something good, that too makes us feel guilty because we feel we don't deserve good things. When we are given a gift, our conscious mind wants it, but the subconscious feels that we are not worthy of it. We feel guilty for receiving the gift, and by feeling guilty, we add to that dark halo surrounding the heart chakra. Guilt does not allow us to experience a high-quality life.

Feeling guilty means you are rejecting yourself. And, if we reject ourselves, we unconsciously think everyone is also rejecting us. This creates fear. This energy is spread all around us and others pick up on that energy and also reject us. So when we feel guilty, others reject us.

You are loved as much as you love others.

An enlightened person loves everyone no matter what. It doesn't matter whether you are trustworthy or not, or angry or not— the enlightened person loves you anyway. Existence has created all of us as we are, and loves all of us. Since an enlightened person is one with Existence, he or she loves everyone too.

The more we mature, the more we appreciate everything, and the more people will love us and appreciate us.

There is always one unfortunate event that brings us to the steps of God. This experience changes our lives. It makes us want to find what really matters and that everything else is beside the point. We have to appreciate that unfortunate event. It has helped us to find ourselves.

If we love and value what we do, we will not look outside ourselves for appreciation, value or approval. The moment we look for these things from others, it shows that we don't value ourselves and our work.

A higher culture is created by appreciation. The higher the culture, the more appreciation you will see. The lower the culture, the less appreciation there is. In lower cultures, people are more selfish. They don't show concern or love for others because they are in the lower chakras. They are mostly concerned with their own wants and needs.

We have often heard that every time we are very happy, we will have to pay for it later with unhappiness. This is very true, because everything has to be balanced in Existence. There is a way out of this loop, however. When we feel very happy and excited, we just have to take a moment, close our eyes, and center ourselves. We can even do a couple of deep breaths to come to the moment. This balances the happiness so we don't have to pay for it with unhappiness. Centering and awareness bring appreciation for the happiness. Appreciation is an act that comes from balanced energies. It is amazing how everything in life is so subtle.

Appreciation is maturity.

Ego is a collection
of all the conditionings
that cause us to suffer.

Everybody wants to be happy but nobody is. We might become happy for a while, but then we become unhappy again. The reason for this is because, in the unconscious, we think we don't deserve happiness. Why? It is the same game the conscious and unconscious minds are always playing—what one wants the other doesn't. We want happiness, but most of the times whatever we want in the conscious, its opposite gets created in the unconscious. If you can forget all about desiring happiness, you will be happy because the unconscious won't have to create the opposite. It won't become involved in tricking you into believing that you don't deserve happiness. This is the only way out of this loop.

    The interesting thing is that the unconscious mind is created first. Then the conscious mind is developed. When we are children, the mind is not conscious yet, so whatever we learn goes into the unconscious. As children, we do many things that cause others to tell us, "You are wrong, you are not good enough, and if you want to be loved, you have to be in a certain way." This makes us feel undeserving in our unconscious. First they teach us that we don't deserve, and then they tell us we have to be happy. This is how we fall into the trap of our conscious and unconscious minds. Then for the rest of our lives, we go on wanting things and not getting them— things like happiness, friendship, money, etc. There is a way out of this loop, and that is to drop desiring.

When the conscious and unconscious are in conflict, we become caught in an inner war that makes us want to prove ourselves. When we try to prove something about ourselves, it just shows that deep inside you don't believe in it. When we get opposite messages from the outside as a child, we push down the ones we don't like into the subconscious and we keep the one we like in the conscious. For example, if you find yourself trying to prove you are smart, know that deep down, in the subconscious, you don't feel very smart. Somewhere along the way, you developed a wound around smartness. Maybe your parents or siblings said something that caused you to doubt yourself. Now, because of this wound, the conscious and the unconscious are in opposition with one another. This opposition creates a lack of confidence in you. The definition of confidence is when the conscious and the unconscious are not opposing one another; they are in agreement. When we heal our wounds, we won't worry about smartness anymore. It moves out of both our conscious mind and our subconscious mind, and we no longer have to prove anything.

Getting a big head or becoming egoistic says to others that we think we are better than you. But we just learned this means deep down, we actually think we are worse. This conflict creates the "big head." If the conflict were not there, this subject (smartness) would not even be in our consciousness. Every time we get in trouble with people, it shows that we have a conflict inside and that we are interpreting the outside according to that conflict. We just have to pay attention to what is in the conscious and what it suggests about the subconscious. Everyone gets mixed messages as a child, creating wounds and inner conflict. This is why we are so busy trying to prove that we are better than others.

When the conscious and unconscious are in conflict, we become caught in an inner war that makes us want to prove ourselves. When we try to prove something about ourselves, it just shows that deep inside you don't believe in it. When we get opposite messages from the outside as a child, we push down the ones we don't like into the subconscious and we keep the one we like in the conscious. For example, if you find yourself trying to prove you are smart, know that deep down, in the subconscious, you don't feel very smart. Somewhere along the way, you developed a wound around smartness. Maybe your parents or siblings said something that caused you to doubt yourself. Now, because of this wound, the conscious and the unconscious are in opposition with one another. This opposition creates a lack of confidence in you. The definition of confidence is when the conscious and the unconscious are not opposing one another; they are in agreement. When we heal our wounds, we won't worry about smartness anymore. It moves out of both our conscious mind and our subconscious mind, and we no longer have to prove anything.

Getting a big head or becoming egoistic says to others that we think we are better than you. But we just learned this means deep down, we actually think we are worse. This conflict creates the "big head." If the conflict were not there, this subject (smartness) would not even be in our consciousness. Every time we get in trouble with people, it shows that we have a conflict inside and that we are interpreting the outside according to that conflict. We just have to pay attention to what is in the conscious and what it suggests about the subconscious. Everyone gets mixed messages as a child, creating wounds and inner conflict. This is why we are so busy trying to prove that we are better than others.

The problem is that when the disliking comes to the surface, we reject it. We don't want to admit, or we are not aware yet, that our negativity comes from our own subconscious, from our own stored memories. Because we are unaware, we look for others to blame and we definitely will find them. Our minds fool us and say this person is horrible, he is at fault, and we stay mad at others. We don't see that we are really mad at ourselves for creating this situation. We don't see that in reality it is us making us miserable because our unconscious is wrongly tainting this experience with some wrong notion that we learned as a child and continued to feed as time went by. The mind and the ego are very tricky. They will do everything they can to keep us from clearly seeing ourselves and our conditionings.

Sometimes we use the emotional body to get revenge. Even the act of becoming emotional is a form of revenge. You don't like someone, and you want to get revenge, so you cry or have a temper tantrum to make them pay. In our life, people have said "no" to us as a child, either by rejecting us or mistreating us. Then for the rest of our lives, we want to get revenge against them. They might not even be there anymore, but we get married to someone like them, so we can get our revenge. Basically, we want to get revenge against anyone who says anything we don't like. When we resolve the issue from the past, we get out of this loop, and as a bonus, we won't get emotional as much.

There is always a war going on between our conscious and subconscious minds. What one wants or likes, the other doesn't want or like. Whatever we don't like consciously, for example, worrying, we really like unconsciously. We love to worry. It makes us feel important. The conscious and subconscious always balance each other this way. If we can just accept that we worry, and part of us really likes it, then worrying will drop from both our conscious and unconscious minds, and we won't worry anymore. We won't even think of worrying.

This works with every issue. For example, if you want money, deep in your subconscious, you don't want money. Because of this conflict, money doesn't come in easily. If money does come in, know that the subconscious wants us to have at least one problem at all times. It knows that problems are how we grow. So it could be that you want money and you get it because the subconscious knows that you may have other problems that will help you grow. Having money could become your problem or fear of losing the money can also become your problem. Whatever the problem, the unconscious gives us unlimited opportunities to practice acceptance and let-go. When we understand this deeply, total acceptance arises and we become free of the duality we live in. There are no more problems because the conscious and unconscious are no longer in opposition and the war ends.

The reason we become old is because we resist and worry all the time. By and by, this worrying becomes a habit. It becomes unconscious. So we worry all the time, and we don't even know that we are worrying. With all this worrying, we waste our energy. Our body gets less and less energy and it ages; we become old. If there is acceptance, our energy gets collected and stored, it becomes our power. When we are not using our energy for doing, it turns into love and sharing. When more and more energy piles up, all of a sudden we become delighted. Life becomes fun, all because of acceptance. Acceptance is magic. Resistance and worry ruin us. When we are accepting and loving, others become loving towards us. Life becomes amazing, magical.

The more you worry about getting something, the less of that thing you will get. If you are worried about money, less money will come to you. If you are worried about getting love, you won't get much love. So don't worry and Existence will shower abundance on you.

Worrying is part of the human condition. If we can just not worry that we are worrying, the worrying will drop after a few minutes. Problems start when we worry and we don't like it. When we resist worrying, it becomes chronic. We worry all the time. Worrying gets prolonged because we don't like it and it makes us miserable. If we accept our worrying, it will pass quickly.

Every blessing is divine and all divinity is a blessing. Blessings happen when our energy is not wasted on worrying. They happen when we are in a state of let-go. The energy that was wasted by worrying is available to us when we let go, and this extra energy makes anything we do better.

We always want to move forward and improve in life. Because of this desire, we ruin every moment. The only thing we need to do is to stay in the moment. This is the ultimate improvement. What we consider improvement right now—losing weight, getting a great job, getting straight A's—destroys the moment by creating fear for the future, fear of not gaining something we think we have to achieve. Most of the time, we don't achieve what we want anyway. All we have really achieved is to replace being in the moment with a life full of worry and fear. Really, we want to achieve because we have been conditioned to believe that achievement will make us happy and joyful. But the truth is, if you stay in the moment, you will experience the most amazing time of your life. You will experience happiness, joy and ecstasy.

Expectation, demanding and all the harshness of the ego collectively is called fear. The absence of these leads us to happiness. So when fear is absent, happiness is possible.

Fear helps us to wake up. When you feel fear, you become more alive. Fear contracts the soul; the soul becomes concentrated. Its energy becomes strong. So don't be afraid of fear. Use it to become awake.

The moment you feel yourself
wanting to run, to escape,
that is a powerful opportunity
for transformation. Instead of
escaping, direct that energy to
the problem and transformation
will happen.

If you can catch your ego in action, it will step aside. When you catch it, the ego says, "There is no place for me here. This person is smarter than I am." When you can't catch your ego, it says, "I am smarter than he is. I can do anything I want." Then the ego runs wild and makes you miserable. The ego is very cunning. If you catch it, it will serve you. If you don't, you will serve it. And since the ego is very smart, it is good to have it on your side.

As long as we focus on the outside world instead of our inner world, we fall apart a lot. We go up and down emotionally with the slightest changes from outside. If someone smiles at us or compliments us, we feel happy, but if they get angry with us, we become sad or angry until something else happens and another reaction comes up. If we succeed at something, again we are happy, we feel good, but if we fail, we will be miserable. When we focus on the inside world, we are more interested in looking at our conditionings and beliefs that cause us to respond the way we do to the outside world. We look for deeper understandings of our responses to things, so we can become free of this roller coaster of likes and dislikes we live on. The day that the inner world becomes more important than the outer, we become totally centered and nothing bothers us anymore. We live in love regardless of what is happening around us.

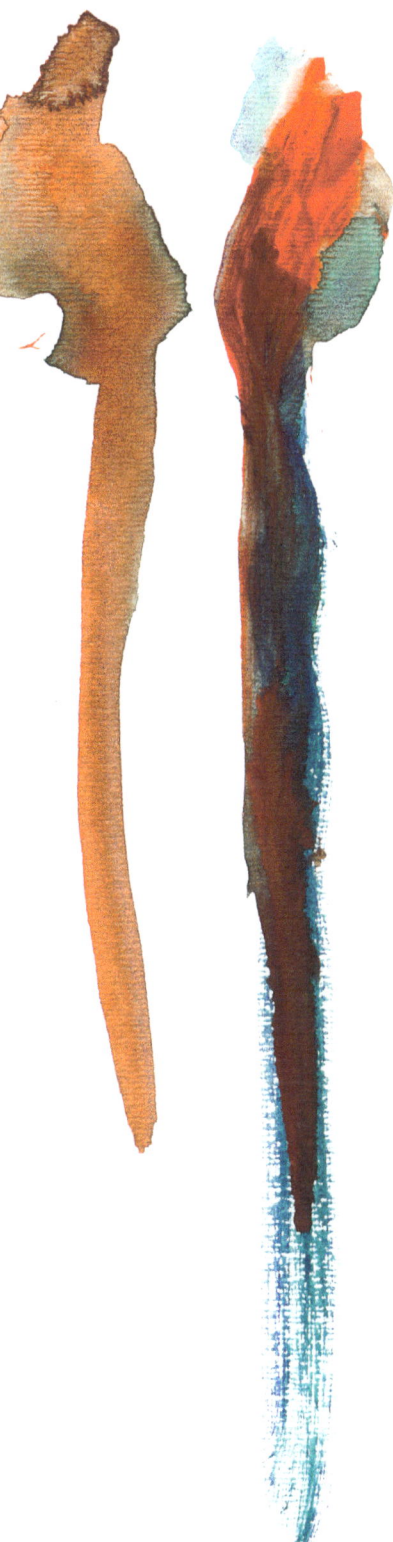

Every time we get upset, remember that only the ego gets upset. Also remember the ego is like a thief; if you catch it red-handed, it will stop.

If we could only see that our misery comes from within us, we could change it quickly. But the fact is that we don't see this. We always want to blame others. We don't look deeper and see that we are the reason for our misery. We divert the problem to others, so we stay ignorant and suffer. And if for some reason, the person or the reason for our current misery goes away, we instantly replace them with someone or something else. We keep ourselves busy with others. We don't bother to look at our own beliefs and conditionings that create these problems in the first place. Just looking and seeing that the problem's source is in us is enough for it to change. So let's look inside instead of outside and drop this life of misery and suffering. Let's live a life of joy and delight instead.

Witnessing is very important because when we witness, we bring energy to our soul. Our energy moves inward instead of outward, or to the mind. The more energy that comes to the soul, the more awake it becomes until one day it awakens totally and we become enlightened. When enlightenment happens, the energy of the soul overflows. At this point witnessing is not needed anymore because the soul is fully awake. Witnessing is only a tool for awakening the soul.

The mind makes us miserable by creating negative thoughts all the time. Then it tricks us into thinking that our misery is other people's fault. So we blame others constantly. If we understand how we create our own misery, dropping the negative becomes easy. When we see how damaging the mind is, we will want to drop it. This makes dropping the mind easier. It's like garbage. When you have garbage in your house, you want to get rid of it, and you do.

Anytime people are in anguish and suffering, it is because either they have not understood something or they have misunderstood. They have missed the deeper understanding of the love of Existence that is happening.

In the moment of understanding, our conditionings melt away. When we deeply understand something, we come out of the mind and connect with our soul or the Beyond. The understanding brings us to the moment. Because our conditionings are the mind, they melt away. Our conditionings are all the things we have been taught.

In the old days, the majority of people were not advanced. They were not as subtle and their understanding was not as developed as it is today. That is why obeying was necessary. A small group of people would decide for everybody, even in one's personal affairs. But today man has become more and more advanced, so we all have to decide for ourselves. Even when we consult with a source that we accept and trust, we still have to measure that advice against our own understanding before we put it into practice. We feel a certain freedom in this process.

When a mystic competes, he feels bad because he thinks competition goes against mysticism. But there is one thing we need to know: today's mysticism is different from that of older times. Back then, life was very simple and basic. If you wanted to work on yourself, you went to a monastery. All you needed was food and shelter. Today is different. We live in a complicated world surrounded by millions of people. We need strong male energy to support our inner path. We need to learn to grow in life, not avoiding them. In those days, working on yourself, or self-realization, was only for certain people. Today many people want to practice self-awareness. Even if we had the opportunity to go to a monastery to work on ourselves, for most, it would be a temporary situation. We would still have to return to our complicated lives and learn how to stay centered.

    Competition is one element of male, and there is nothing wrong with it. We see someone who is better than we are and we want to become better too. It brings strength to the male. It only becomes a problem when we don't like that we are competing. We want to hide it. This makes us weak and weakness leads to jealousy. So jealousy happens when unconsciously we think we are weak and others are better than us. We envy them. If we understand that there is nothing wrong with competition, then we won't be jealous any more. In Nature, you see all kinds of competition; what you don't see is jealousy. Competition is natural. Jealousy is a byproduct of not understanding competition.

If you understand, you can be humble. Only people who understand are generous, because they understand that things or possessions are worthless. Because of this, their ego doesn't get puffed up about their generosity.

Any desiring creates blockages in the chakra related to those desires. Financial desires work from the first chakra, creating blockages there. Desiring love from others creates blockages in the heart. When a chakra becomes blocked, the vastness of that center becomes restricted. If it is blocked for a long time, the energy that passes through that center to the body also becomes restricted, gradually leading to the malfunctioning of the various organs and areas of the body associated with that center.

So anywhere we have desires, we create blockages. Our culture tells us that if you desire something and you work hard for it, you will get it. This is true, but the only reason we have to work so hard is because of the blockages our desires create. This is why we believe that to reach any goal requires hard work. You see this in life all the time. One person has to work really hard to get a certain task done, while someone else breezes through it effortlessly. It all depends on where we are blocked.

If we look at this in depth, we see that a desire for power, which happens in the third chakra, creates blockages in the third chakra. These blockages then restrict the energy that passes through that chakra, actually making it much harder to become powerful. In fact, we become less powerful. Or, if we have been conditioned from childhood that money is the most important thing, our first chakra will desire money all the time, creating blockages there. Then less money or not enough money will result. Even if we make good money, that money won't give us blessings or happiness. We will always be greedy for more and feel miserable. Our childhood conditionings create blockages in the first chakra, and now our desires and worrying about money as adults make it even worse. With blockages, we can't feel satisfied. Satisfaction comes from a clean chakra; dissatisfaction comes from a blocked chakra.

When we get bothered by other people's behavior, it shows that we have blockages in our soul. What we feel about others is really what is happening inside us. It has nothing to do with the outside. The outside can trigger things inside, but nothing more. When we look deeper, we'll see that every time we feel bad, it's because we feel guilty about something. Guilt makes us feel bad. Basically, the main issue in our emotional body is guilt. The reason we have so much guilt is that we think we are doing everything, that we are responsible. We simply don't have trust for Existence; we don't believe that Existence is in charge, so we blame ourselves. We say things to ourselves like, "I didn't do a good job. I should be better. I should have said something! Why did I do that?" The list goes on and on. We are experts at beating ourselves up. Or we avoid looking at ourselves by blaming others.

 The reason for all this is the mind. The mind is a machine that only keeps records of the negative past. It takes these records and projects them into the future. When we are in the mind, we worry and cannot trust. The only way to get out of this exploitation by the mind is to become aware. When we are aware, we don't identify with the mind. We come to the moment. In the moment, there is no negativity, no guilt, and no mind. In the moment, we move into ecstasy. We become one with Existence. At these times, trust happens on its own. All we need to do is become more aware.

"Drink a cup of tea
with awareness
every day."

There is almost always a struggle between men and women in relationships. Everyone is avoiding domination by the other, but the only reason we get dominated by the other is because we also want to dominate them. Everyone tries to dominate, that is just the nature of the ego. So the struggle is not caused by the others wanting to dominate us, the struggle comes from not understanding how the ego works. If you stop dominating others, others will also stop dominating you.

Domination happens in the third chakra. If your third chakra is strong, you dominate others; if your third chakra is weak, you get dominated. Either way, you are in the third chakra. If someone is in the first or second chakra, others might decide for them or tell them what to do, but they won't feel dominated. Everything related to domination happens in the third chakra. So if you feel dominated, remember that you are coming from the same place as the other guy, just from the opposite side of the coin. He is no better or worse than you are.

As we grow, we become more and more gentle, to the point where we see that even judgment is harmful to others. The mind is so crowded with judgment. If we don't judge, the mind stops.

At its peak, the third chakra starts helping others. When we help others, we make them dependent on us. We want them to need us. This comes from a longing in humans for unity. We want to become one with others. In the third chakra, we only know how to do this by making others dependent on us. This basic need for unity arises the moment we are born, when our parents and society start developing an identity for us that is separate from others. Then we suffer for the rest of our lives because of this separation. But this separation is an illusion. We are all one, and the day we realize this, our suffering will subside.

When we go to the heart chakra, the fourth chakra, we understand that everything is done by Existence and not us. As long as we still have blockages in the third chakra, however, we believe that we are responsible, and we should be careful not to hurt others. This is because when we are in the third chakra, we don't have love yet. We are still capable of hurting others. Once love happens and the fourth chakra opens, we cannot hurt anyone anymore. This is why, once we reach the heart chakra, Existence allows us to understand that we are not responsible, that whatever we do is done by Existence through us. If people in the third chakra understood that everything is done by Existence, they would abuse this understanding. They would hurt others and then say, "It was Existence, not me." Everything in Existence is so impeccable that until we are in the fourth chakra, we won't be able to see that Existence is in charge. We will still believe we are in charge. This is divine wisdom in action.

Awareness is when all of a sudden you remember something. It is a remembrance. It could be something simple, like you become aware that you have a doctor's appointment tomorrow, or something deeper, like a repressed memory or a belief system that causes you to act or react in certain ways. Awareness means paying attention and with paying attention, things make sense. Awareness brings things from the unconscious into the conscious mind. It gives us clarity.

We talk a lot about all the things the mind does, but in reality, the mind only does one thing—it separates. It separates everything— day and night, black and white, good and bad, and on and on. It separates people. We are all one, but the mind separates us. It is as if all the cells of our body had minds of their own and started disagreeing and judging each other, and fighting among themselves. Some would become greedy, hoarding all the blood and oxygen for themselves; others would refuse to hang out and communicate with certain types of cells. Can you imagine? Our bodies would be a mess. All this mess goes with separation. Because those cells don't have minds, they really cooperate with one another. They get along beautifully. We are all cells of one body, the body of Existence, and we could also get along beautifully if we could just see our minds and not fall into their games of separation.

Growth and change are two different things. Growth happens inside, change happens on the periphery. Wanting to change your personality is not growth. Your personality has been tailored by Existence for this specific body and soul. So instead of trying to change your personality, use it to know yourself in order to grow. Watch everything that happens in you and bring awareness and light to it.

We have been around for billions of years and we will be around for billions more. We will be always here. We will be here for eternity. There is no end. The mind thinks there is a beginning and there is an end, but the truth is that we are eternal, so there is no need to rush. If you find out something negative about yourself, be happy. Do not try to change it. Do not try to accept it. Do not put pressure on yourself or get angry at yourself. Don't hate yourself or others. You don't need to defend yourself or to bury your head in the sand trying to ignore that this negative thing exists. Instead, just watch when that negative thing comes up again.

We are here, and we are not in a rush. This rush inside us is from the world. We approach growth like going to school, believing that we have to rush and get good grades and learn a lot right now. This is why there is so much rush in the world. We think we have only one life, so we have to hurry up and do, do, do, do to take advantage of the time we have. All this is nonsense. Relax, watch, and be aware of your negativities. You don't need to understand anything. You don't need to alter anything. Just watch for now. Understanding comes when you have watched long enough. When you watch, by and by, you go deeper, and understanding comes.

We have so many repressed emotions and tensions in us, but we are so used to them, we don't feel them anymore. When we become more aware, we come out of our habits. Awareness basically means coming out of our habits and seeing things clearly. When this happens, it is truly as if we are seeing things for the first time. Things that were always there, but we were unaware of, start bothering us. This is great because it motivates us to finally do something about it, to relax, and center ourselves in order to get rid of these tensions. If we are unaware of our emotions and tensions, we will never feel we need to center ourselves.

Focusing and centering are two different phenomena. Focusing involves setting your mind on just one thing, paying attention to one thing. Focusing creates tension. Thinking is focusing, and thinking makes you tense. But when centering yourself, you relax. Your tension becomes less. When you listen to music from a centered place as opposed to focusing on it, you become one with the music.

As you become more aware, you need to center yourself more, because with awareness you become more aware of lots and lots of tension. This is bothersome. You need to become more relaxed. Meditation is centering.

Acceptance is our bridge to the Beyond. It takes us from misery and suffering to joy and let-go, but acceptance only happens if you are centered. We cannot accept directly. First we relax; then our awareness grows, which makes centering necessary, and finally acceptance follows. With focusing awareness lessens. So the more you use the mind, the more unaware you become. The more meditation you do, the more aware you become, because the mind slows down with meditation. When we become aware, we can see everything clearly and acceptance comes. If you are not aware, you cannot see things clearly and you cannot accept. Acceptance only happens through relaxation and awareness.

When we are unaware, our repressed negativity comes up. Then we act accordingly and mistreat ourselves and others. Humans are unaware of themselves because they are too close to themselves. When they get close to someone else, they become unaware of that person too. That's when a lot of problems start in relationships. We start mistreating the people close to us just like we do to ourselves. The more distant people are, the more aware they are of one another, and the more they respect each other. Distance allows us to be more aware and see things more clearly. The more distant someone is, the less we take them for granted.

Everybody feels like a loser deep inside because everyone has died and come back again. Every time we die, we feel that we have wasted our life because we missed becoming aware, becoming enlightened. Only people who become aware start looking for why they are really here. If you are still trying to win, you will continue down the wrong path to the end of this life too, only realizing too late why you are really here. Even if you win, you will still encounter this feeling of being a loser. This is actually a great thing, because when you win and it still does nothing to stop that loser feeling, you will stop expecting that anything but awareness and enlightenment will satisfy you. If you have yet to win, you might always carry the hope that winning will take away this feeling like a loser.

When our awareness grows, we may still fall into the negativities of the lower chakras, but when we are even more aware, going to the lower chakras brings healing and cleansing to those chakras.

The more mature we are, the more we have acceptance for negativity. Maturity means looking at negativity without getting caught up in it. It gives us a sense of freedom, of let-go. We see how negativity helps us to look at life more deeply. That is basically what growth means, looking at life more deeply. And why is growth important for us? Because when we grow, we expand our limits in every direction— financially, emotionally, creatively, in our careers, in our relationships … and we feel more joy. We experience all of this in the world of let-go. With this deeper understanding of negativity, things won't bother us as much. We will see how positivity and negativity *both* are the nourishment and love of Existence. Then we will have power over negativity instead of negativity having power over us.

The source of disliking others comes from not liking ourselves. We practice this not liking ourselves every day. We judge ourselves constantly and dislike many things we do. We are so good at it that we often aren't aware of how much we do it. It has become an unconscious activity—constantly beating ourselves up for the things we don't like about ourselves. If we stop beating up ourselves, we will like other people and different situations also. How do we stop judging ourselves? We need to become more aware. We can do this by doing simple exercises to increase our awareness. For example drink tea with awareness. We pay attention to the tiniest movements of our hands when drinking. Focus on the taste of the tea in your mouth. Its aroma. Feel the warmth of the cup in your hands. Really focus on this simple act of drinking the tea. When we become total, we come to the here and now; we come to the moment. So drinking tea with awareness brings us to the moment.

When our awareness grows, most of our habits stop automatically. When we can see our judgments and all the things we do that hurt us, we have the power to stop them. Seeing something is the real challenge. So just drink your tea with awareness.

The reason men and women are attracted to each other is because in love-making, the woman becomes totally female. That female energy is more subtle than her usual female energy. The man becomes totally male, and his male energy is also more subtle because of totality than his usual male energy. These two energies melt into each other creating an explosion that stops the mind. It is like a mini-enlightenment. That is why there is so much attraction to sex. But sex is not required for this melting to happen. If a man and a woman do anything together with totality, this explosion and stopping of the mind can happen. They can eat a meal together or look at the sunset. All that is needed is totality.

There are things we do that bring our inner male and female together and some other things that separate them. When you think only of yourself—whether you are thinking, "Poor me" or, "That guy's a jerk"—your male and female separate. Thinking is male and the self (the ego) is also male. With so much male, there is no room for the female, so she steps aside. In general, the female is relaxed, she feels fulfilled. Without the female, the male becomes aggressive and starts fighting. He sucks the life out of the moment. The moment you relax and don't worry about the self, this division drops. The male and female join and you become happy, excited. The male joined with the female breathes life into the moment. We call a man whose male and female are balanced, a gentleman. He is truly a gentle man. It is a beautiful concept.

Watching is one important way to bring our male and female together. Watching means paying attention, looking; it means being more total with what we are doing and experiencing. Our doing is male; paying attention to our doing is female. So when we pay attention to our doing, the male and female join, they become one, and we become centered and balanced.

Understanding is another way to bring our male and female together. With deep understanding, awareness comes in, and immediately we become centered. The male and female join and we feel immensely alive and joyful.

It is important to remember that when we talk about male and female, we are talking about the male and female inside each and every one of us, regardless of gender.

A woman gets interested in a man because her own male energy is not strong enough or she has a lot of male energy, but is not in touch with it. When we become more and more aware of the opposite energy inside us, we need the opposite sex less and less. When we have this awareness, even if there is a relationship with the opposite sex, it becomes more fluent and easy because it is not out of need. It becomes a delight. How can we become aware of the opposite energy inside us? By watching and seeing it when it arises, over and over again. Make a note for yourself, reminding you to watch for your opposite side. Put it on the wall and look at it every day. By and by, if you stick with it, it will happen—you will become aware of this opposite energy within you. The trick is to not forget to watch. We easily get distracted and forget about the essentials.

It is very interesting how the male and female are related to the conscious and the unconscious mind. If you have more male energy, your conscious is male and your unconscious is female. If you have more female energy, your conscious is female and your unconscious is male. In general, we act most often out of the energy of our conscious mind. If it is male, we are more male. But this is not always the case. Different situations bring out different energies in us. Depending on the situation, our energy will change from male to female and back again-often. What this really means is that we only use one side of our brain at a time.

    If our male and female energies are both strong and they are at peace with one another, they become one and we have access to both sides of our brain at once. We don't swing between male and female. This is what enlightenment is. At this point, we have the energy of the Beyond. We can still drop into male or female energy if we choose, but mostly we are balanced and in ecstasy all the time.

Our depth or the Beyond is pure female, our surface is more male. When the depth and the surface meet, balance happens. This is what happens with awareness exercises; for example, when we move our hand with awareness. The movement is male, the awareness is female. The more we do this exercise, the more our male and female become friends, and the more balanced we are.

Also, when we pay attention to our hand, the energy goes into the hand instead of the mind. In this way, we bypass the mind. Our energy is so used to going to the mind that we are stuck in our mind most of the time. In the mind, there are thoughts and attached to thoughts are emotions. If we divert our energy to the body, by and by, the mind will subside; we bypass thoughts and emotions and become free. We become simple and enjoy the let go so much.

We live in a dual world: we need to keep balancing the opposites. For example, if we are happy, at some point we will become sad. Existence balances the two opposites. We need these ups and downs to grow.

What does it really mean to go to hell? It means you become total in suffering, which cleanses your karmas. Suffering cleanses all the negative accumulations of the past that darken our soul. No fire or bomb can affect your soul; only the fire of suffering burns karma. After suffering, we become clean and refreshed. While we are in the body, when karma comes out of the capillaries of the soul, we feel pain and suffering. If we gain deeper understanding, we can cleanse our karma without pain. Deep understanding cleanses us automatically, so there is no need for hell or suffering. All we have to do is to expand our understanding, and our life will become a journey full of delight and joy.

When we die, all karma is cleansed from our soul. This is another gift of Existence to us. Of course, our account with Existence remains open, and since life is about growth, we get reborn into a family that creates the same environment, or the same karma, that we had at the end of our last lifetime. We pick up right where we left off. Existence is all about love. All we need to do is to gain more understanding. With deeper understanding, we will see the love of Existence in absolutely everything.

Ironically, in order to become enlightened, we need karma, or negative energy. Negative energy puts us under pressure, and we need that pressure to grow. Enlightenment has to be earned, so Existence gives us the opportunity to grow by providing all sorts of negativity in our lives. Basically, growth means we feel pressure and then at some point we let go and the pressure goes away. We do this over and over again until we eventually learn to be in a let-go state all the time. We become a free spirit. We become enlightened. Then negativity—any negativity—doesn't affect us anymore. Until we reach this let-go state, though, we are given lots of opportunities to feel pressure and grow, and we have to be thankful for them.

Anytime we are not authentic, we get other people's karma. For example, we see someone we don't like very much and we say, "Oh, it's so nice to see you." Or people have gone bankrupt and you think they kind of deserved it, but when you see them you say, "Oh, I am so sorry. I feel terrible for you!" When we do this, we get their karma. That is also Existence's love, because the reason that person has gone bankrupt is because they have a chunk of karma blocking their soul. When we take their karma, we get heavy, but they become lighter. With more openness in their soul, they can start rebuilding their lives.

This works out well for them, but we need to be more aware for our own sake. We need to make sure that we are authentic all the time. If we see someone we don't like, we don't have to say, "Oh, so good to see you." We could say, "Good morning. I hope you have a good day." Or to the person who is going bankrupt and you think they deserve it, instead of saying, "Oh, I feel terrible for you," just say, "It must be really hard. I hope you feel better soon." Be as authentic as possible, because when you are authentic, you avoid lots of negativity and your life becomes lighter and more joyful. Even if sometimes you have to say something that you don't mean to avoid hurting someone's feelings, know that Existence wants you to get that karma. In order for us to grow, we need a certain amount of karma, and if we don't have it, Existence sees to it that we get it. Even karma is the love of Existence.

Our soul has capillaries, just like our circulatory system, for energy to travel through. In the body, there are places where several of these capillaries come together, or intersect. There are also places where the threadlike strands of our nervous system intersect. A meridian point is where an intersection of the capillaries of the soul aligns with an intersection of the threads of the nervous system. They sit one on top of the other at the same point. When we get sad or angry or upset in any way, negative energy is created and travels through the capillaries of our soul. Because this energy is coarse, it gets stuck in the meridian points. It is too dense to pass through these intersections. The result is that energy cannot get through those capillaries anymore, and the part of nervous system that is aligned with these capillaries becomes weak because energy cannot travel through closed capillaries. These stuck negative energies act like toxins in the body, creating pain and discomfort, and over the long term, disease is created in the areas near that point. The opposite is also true. Toxins in the body can weaken the soul's circulatory system, creating negative energy in our Emotional Body. For example, you eat junk food and you feel bad physically; then, all of a sudden, you become depressed.

Negative energy entering the body can get stored in fat cells. If we have less fat, these negative energies affect the body directly. The body can become extremely sensitive and prone to discomfort. For example, putting up with things pushes negative energies into the body. If we have more fat, we have more room to store this negative energy, so up to a certain point, it won't bother us as much. If we have less fat, our body will tend to fall apart easily. This falling apart is a good thing. It is Existence telling us to do something about all the "putting up with" that we are doing. It is telling us to sort things out, to open things up and talk about what is bothering us. It is telling us to do something about our issues.

Every time you hear laughter, it is a sign from the universe for you to also laugh. When you hear laughter, laugh. Laughter meditation is good for you. It helps get you out of the heaviness of your mind and into your heart. At some point during your day, when you have the time or when you hear someone laughing, start laughing. Laugh for twenty minutes. Be aware that laughter meditation may make you feel angry at some point. As we know, earth is a place of dualities, of opposites and the opposite of laughter is anger. So when we laugh, anger may come up to keep us in balance. This is a very good combo.

As children we were told anger is bad. Anger isn't bad. In fact, it is good. It is very healthy. Without it, humanity would die. Two things are absolutely necessary for humanity— anger and laughter. Society is very cunning. It tells us that anger is bad and in saying so, it keeps us angry all the time. Anger is good especially when we accept it. When we accept it, when we are happy with it because we know it is necessary, it comes and goes quickly. When we think anger is bad, if it comes up, we hate it. We don't accept our anger, so it sticks with us. It goes straight to our subconscious and festers. If we allow it, it cleanses the subconscious.

Anger is the healthiest thing there is. Get angry every day for ten minutes. Just sit and feel anger. If you do this every day for three or four weeks, after a month, your deeply repressed anger will be gone. You will just have normal anger that arises throughout the day to keep you balanced. That old rotten repressed anger will be gone. When we work with mysticism, we keep clearing away the roots of our conditionings so we can be free. Anger is one of the bigger roots and a key player in why we beat ourselves up.

People are afraid of responsibility because almost everyone as a child was given something to do and failed to do it properly. They gave us something to carry; we dropped it and they yelled at us. This becomes our memory of responsibility. Then for the rest of our lives, we try to avoid taking responsibility. We are afraid that if we accept responsibility, we will fail again. If we do become responsible for something, it becomes really heavy for us.

Responsibility by itself, with no negative memories of the past, with no resistance, is the easiest thing to do. It's the most fun thing to do, the most rewarding thing to do, and it is the most fulfilling thing to do. The only reason we don't like responsibility is because of resistance created by our past memories. This resistance doesn't allow us to become total when taking responsibility, so it becomes very hard. If we can see this resistance to responsibility in every aspect of our lives, and consciously bring understanding to it, realizing that the past is gone, we will relieve ourselves of that heaviness. We will accept responsibility with a freshness. We will enjoy responsibility, and everything will work out beautifully. Life becomes so fun.

When we start taking responsibility, we will see that by taking responsibility, we are taking a heavy load off our shoulders. When we don't take responsibility, we hate ourselves and we feel guilty. On the other hand, every time we accept responsibility with no resistance, life becomes so fulfilling, so joyful. When we take total responsibility, it is the experience of Enlightenment. Even if we don't become enlightened in this lifetime, we become so refined that our next life becomes much easier.

When we give with our heart, we get back one thousand-fold. We have heard this before, but how does it work? The heart is where the energy of the Beyond descends, so when we give with our hearts open, the energy of the Beyond is with us. When we give with our heart, miracles happen. If you give when you are in the lower chakras, you won't get anything back. You might even lose. In lower chakras, we give grudgingly, with resistance or out of obligation. Because of this, the energy of the Beyond is not involved, so we don't get anything back. In the heart, getting back is inevitable.

When we don't have faith in ourselves,
we don't believe in miracles.

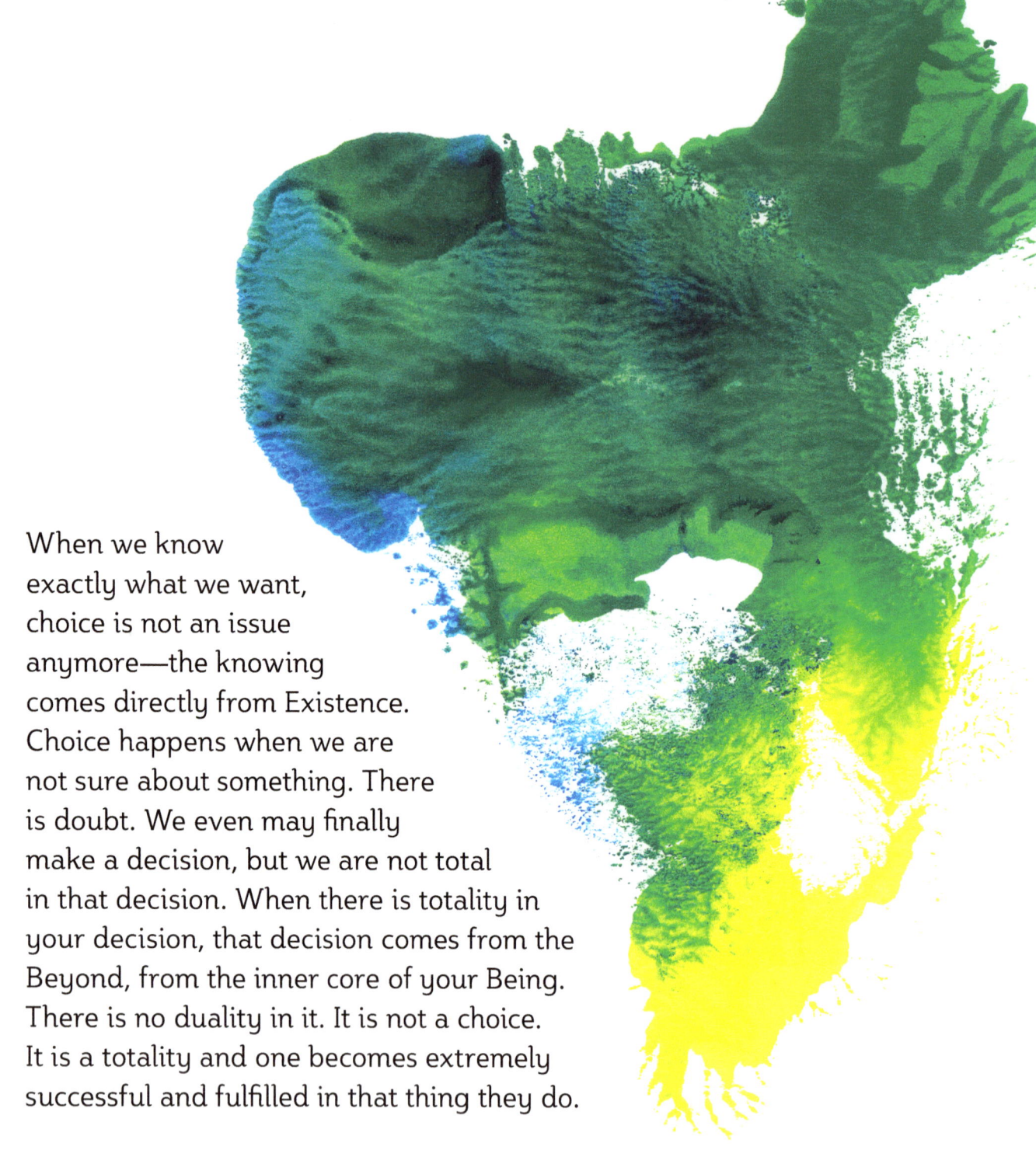

When we know exactly what we want, choice is not an issue anymore—the knowing comes directly from Existence. Choice happens when we are not sure about something. There is doubt. We even may finally make a decision, but we are not total in that decision. When there is totality in your decision, that decision comes from the Beyond, from the inner core of your Being. There is no duality in it. It is not a choice. It is a totality and one becomes extremely successful and fulfilled in that thing they do.

If you are bored in life, having fun takes you high. You get a glimpse of the Beyond, but then you come down again. If you have experienced the Beyond directly, through opening your heart or from a deep understanding, then having fun becomes pale compared to the ecstasy of the Beyond. Leisure becomes low unless you bring the quality of the Beyond to it. Then you touch the Beyond while you are having fun. Basically, everything you do becomes divine and ecstatic with the Beyond.

Anytime you feel
freedom and let go,
it is because something
has helped you to
touch the Beyond.

You are reading this book just to hear the messages of the Beyond. Every time we hear the messages of the Beyond, they open our hearts. When our hearts open, loving one another happens.

GLOSSARY

AWARENESS: In normal life we usually are not aware of our Being. We only associate ourselves with our thoughts. Awareness means becoming aware of our Being by stopping the mind. We can stop the mind with meditation, focusing, or experiencing a moment of deep joy or understanding.

BODIES OF THE SOUL: We humans have seven different layers in our soul. We call them the bodies of the soul. The physical body is at the center of these layers, while all the other bodies move outwards from this center like the ripples created by throwing a stone in a lake.

> **FIRST BODY: Physical Body**
>
> **SECOND BODY: Etheric Body** – The etheric body extends about one inch beyond our physical body. All the chakras are part of this body.
>
> **THIRD BODY: Emotional Body** – The emotional body extends about three feet out from the physical body. It is the body that stores our emotions.
>
> **FOURTH BODY: Mental Body** – The mental body extends beyond the emotional body, but the extent to which it and the rest of the bodies do so depends upon our spiritual advancement. The mental body carries our thoughts and relates to the mind.
>
> **FIFTH BODY: Bliss Body** – Where ecstasy resides. The bliss body contains the information of the past and is about hearing the voice of Existence.
>
> **SIXTH BODY: Spiritual Body** – The spiritual body contains the information of the future. It is about seeing the Beyond.
>
> **SEVENTH BODY: Nirvanic Body** – This body is about joining with the universe, becoming one with God.

CHAKRAS: The chakras are centers of the soul. They sit in the spine and head and direct different aspects of being.

FIRST CHAKRA: The first chakra is primarily concerned with survival issues, money, the instinctual. The way the first chakra operates is through attachment.

SECOND CHAKRA: The second chakra is more about pleasure, sex, and the emotions.

THIRD CHAKRA: This chakra relates to power, control, and the mental body, the mind.

FOURTH CHAKRA: The heart center is concerned with trust, letting go, love and acceptance.

FIFTH CHAKRA: This chakra is involved in expressing and hearing: specifically, hearing the voice of Existence.

SIXTH CHAKRA: The sixth chakra is also called the third eye, which sees the hidden aspects of Existence, aspects the other five senses cannot sense.

SEVENTH CHAKRA: The seventh chakra relates to dropping attachments to the material world totally, living in the divine with absolute freedom.

CLEANSING: Getting rid of the energies that are not subtle *(karma)* and are blocking our chakras, causing us emotional pain, discomfort, and misery.

CONCENTRATION: Means focusing. Sometimes meditation and concentration get confused. Concentration is the first step to meditation. We use the mind to beat the mind by focusing totally. When we focus totally, we use the mind intensively, so much so that all of a sudden, it stops and meditation happens.

CONDITIONING: Teachings from our parents, teachers, and the society in general that create our belief systems and personality.

CONSCIOUSNESS: The mind is divided into two parts: the part we are aware of called consciousness and a much larger part of which we are not aware, the sub- or unconscious. The subconscious controls much of our feelings and reactions automatically without our really understanding why.

ECSTACY: A state of being where all the darkness of the soul is gone, leaving tremendous satisfaction or joy. Enlightenment is a state of everlasting ecstacy.

ENLIGHTENMENT: Simply put, the individual is in charge of, or has conquered, his ego and is in direct contact with Existence. His consciousness is lit up.

EXISTENCE: Existence includes everything in the universe from the material, animal, and the human to the emotional, mental, energetic—everything. We use this term almost synonymously with God, except that we are not separate from Existence. We are a necessary and vital part of the Whole. It includes the deepest levels of understanding to the most shallow, and includes all aspects of human behavior, regardless of how we judge these behaviors as good or bad, valuable or not valuable. All is essential to the Whole.

GOING TO THE HEART: Being in the heart or going to the heart means our kundalini energy rises from the first chakra up through the spine, passing all the lower chakras as it goes. As we travel higher up this main artery of the soul, the pathways become more subtle. So the energy can only continue to climb based on how subtle it has become. When we are stuck in the lower chakras, we feel that we are not safe enough. We believe that we need to control the things around us. To do this we use the mind. A lot of energy is used by the mind for thinking, which causes emotional pain, unhappiness, and a feeling of heaviness. Feeling love is the key to making the energy subtle enough to climb to the heart chakra and higher, which brings feelings of love, gentleness, and let-go. This is what we call going to the heart.

KARMA: Karma is a negative energy that creates blockages in the soul and the body.

KUNDALINI: The source of our personal energy, sitting in the first chakra. It is also called the energy of our life or the energy of the soul.

MALE/FEMALE: The kundalini energy is broken into two parts, male and female, regardless of whether you are a man or a woman. The left side of the body is governed by the female energy and the right side is governed by the male.

MEDITATION: This is a state of no mind, but when we talk about meditation, mostly it means creating situations to help the mind to stop, like sitting in silence and closing the eyes.

PRANA: The energy of Existence that we take in from our surroundings by breathing, eating, etc.

SUBCONSCIOUS (UNCONSCIOUS): Subconscious is below the conscious. Many paths divide the subconscious into subconscious and unconscious, but for general understanding, subconscious and unconscious are the same thing, unless you want to dissect them for different points of understanding. For example, subconscious is the new material that has been put in the basement of our mind. Unconscious is the older material, even from our last lifetime.

TOTALITY: This is becoming as intense, as completely focused as possible in whatever we are doing or feeling.

TRANSFORMATION: Transformation is when the mind stops, for whatever reason, and in result some blockages open up. Deep understanding will cause the mind to step aside. The ego also steps aside when the mind stops and our kundalini energy moves to the heart or higher, allowing for deep peace, joy, and ecstasy. Consequently, we experience inner opening and change.

Paintings by Sharam
View and purchase giclée prints

Visit:
SharamLove.com

www.ingramcontent.com/pod-product-compliance
Lightning Source LLC
Chambersburg PA
CBHW041528220426
43671CB00002B/24